# Fairy the Friendly Fawn

## *From Rescue to Rehabilitation to Release*

Lori Klisman Ellis

**Arkett Publishing**
New Milford, Connecticut USA

# Fairy the Friendly Fawn
## *From Rescue to Rehabilitation to Release*

### Lori Klisman Ellis

published by

𝕒

ARKETT PUBLISHING
division of Arkettype
PO Box 36, Gaylordsville, CT 06755
860-350-4007 • Fax 860-355-3970
www.local-author.com

ISBN 979-8-8692-7013-9

Printed in USA

# INTRODUCTION

Located in the beautiful eastern Canadian wilderness, **Wild Hearts Animal Sanctuary** is a wonderful place of refuge dedicated to helping and healing animals in need. The sanctuary offers injured, orphaned, neglected, and abused animals a second chance at life, and gives them a safe place to call home. Jean Francois "Jeff" Letendre devotes himself to rescuing and rehabilitating the most vulnerable animals, creating a haven for them on the sanctuary's 1,000 acres of pristine landscape with meandering rivers, streams, wetlands, majestic waterfalls, mountains, and forest. Animals at the sanctuary receive great care during their rescue and rehabilitation, and they are never sold, traded, killed, or used for medical testing. Animals here can live in peace.

Go to **https://www.thewildhearts.org/** to learn more about Wild Hearts Animal Sanctuary.

# DEDICATION

I dedicate this book to all the kind and compassionate people around the world who rescue and rehabilitate animals. Thank you for saving these vulnerable creatures, and for giving them a second chance to live a healthy, wonderful life.

*Jeff and Fairy*

# Fairy the Friendly Fawn

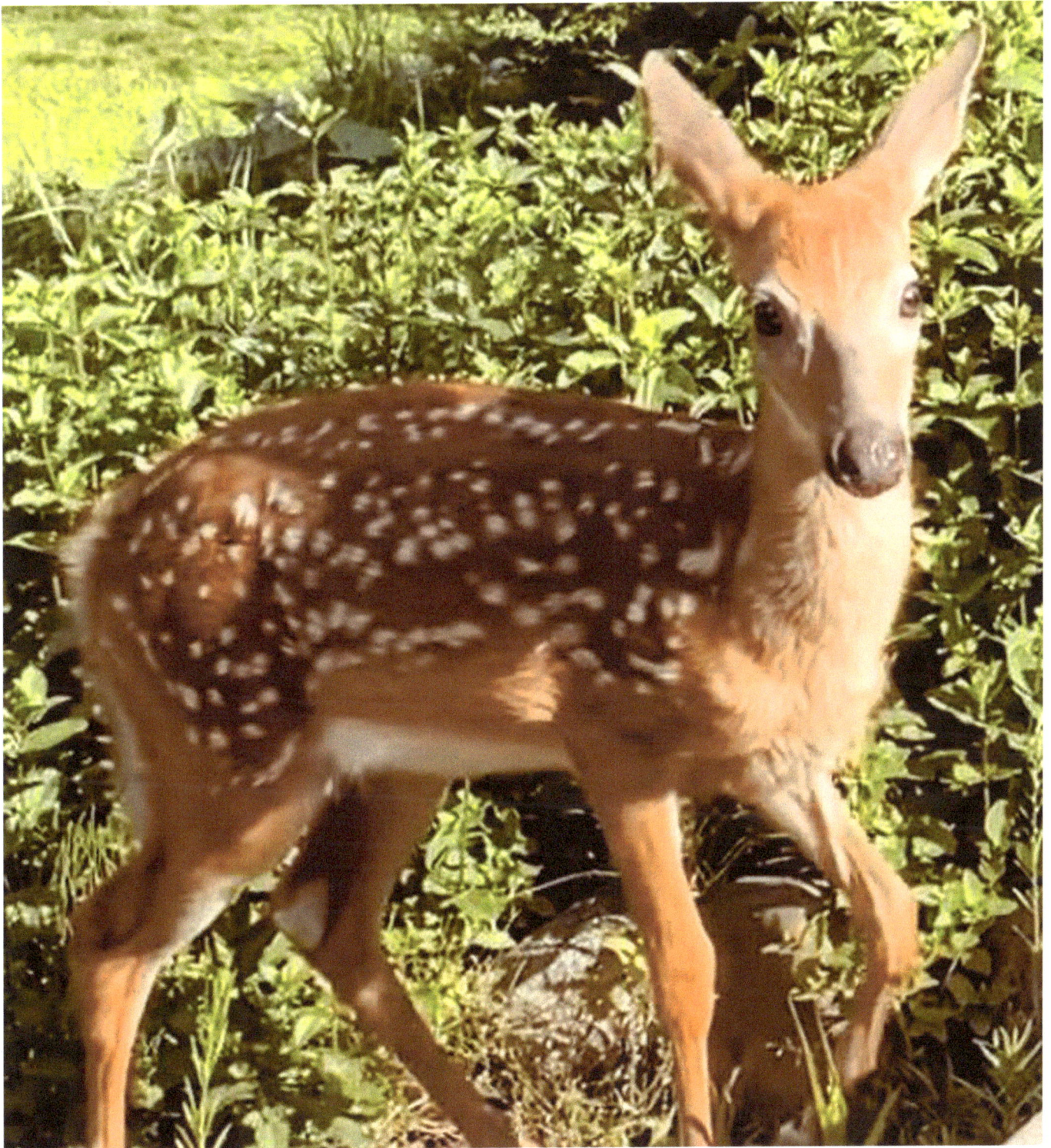

In the majestic land of Ontario, Canada, in the summer of 2023, a sweet baby fawn was born. But tragedy soon struck. Her mom was killed, leaving the little fawn an orphan who had to fend for herself. She wandered the wilderness alone, meandering through a forest lush with trees, waterfalls, and mountains. Imagine her surprise when she met a prince!

Prince Jeff helps orphaned and injured animals, and his unexpected meeting with the tiny fawn was simply magical. She was adorable with her small white spots, fluffy white tail, and large, innocent eyes that gazed at her new-found human/dad/prince. Prince Jeff opened his heart and his doors to the sweet fawn, and the two soon became inseparable.

*The fawn was wandering alone in the woods searching for her mom and for help.*

*Fairy was getting good nourishment for the first time since her mom died. In the background is one of Jeff's "love balls," Jenny the orphaned raccoon.*

Prince Jeff decided to call her "Fairy." He slowly approached her to offer some food. Fairy was at first hesitant to accept the bottle filled with plant-based milk formula, but soon the scent was so enticing, and she was so hungry, that she came closer and emptied the bottle within seconds. Prince Jeff went back

to his castle and returned with five more bottles of the luscious formula for ravenous Fairy to guzzle down.

The bond between Fairy and Prince Jeff grew stronger by the day. As Prince Jeff explored the forest, he looked forward to Fairy's daily visits. She would prance toward his castle and he would feed her the nutritious formula. After six months, he began to offer her delicious treats such as apple slices, grapes, and banana chips.

Fairy soon began to follow Prince Jeff on his daily walks in the forest. He would whistle and Fairy would come dancing in the wind toward him. She emanated joy when she was with him. Prince Jeff wanted to give Fairy some of the new opportunities and experiences that her mom would have shown her, so he took her to the flowing river. She listened to the calming sounds and was mesmerized

by the ripples in the water. She was a bit hesitant to immerse herself, but she slowly placed her hoofs in the water and she liked it.

Eventually, Fairy even allowed her prince to pet and brush her fur. She enjoyed his affection. She thought this was pure heaven. "I could get used to this," thought Fairy.

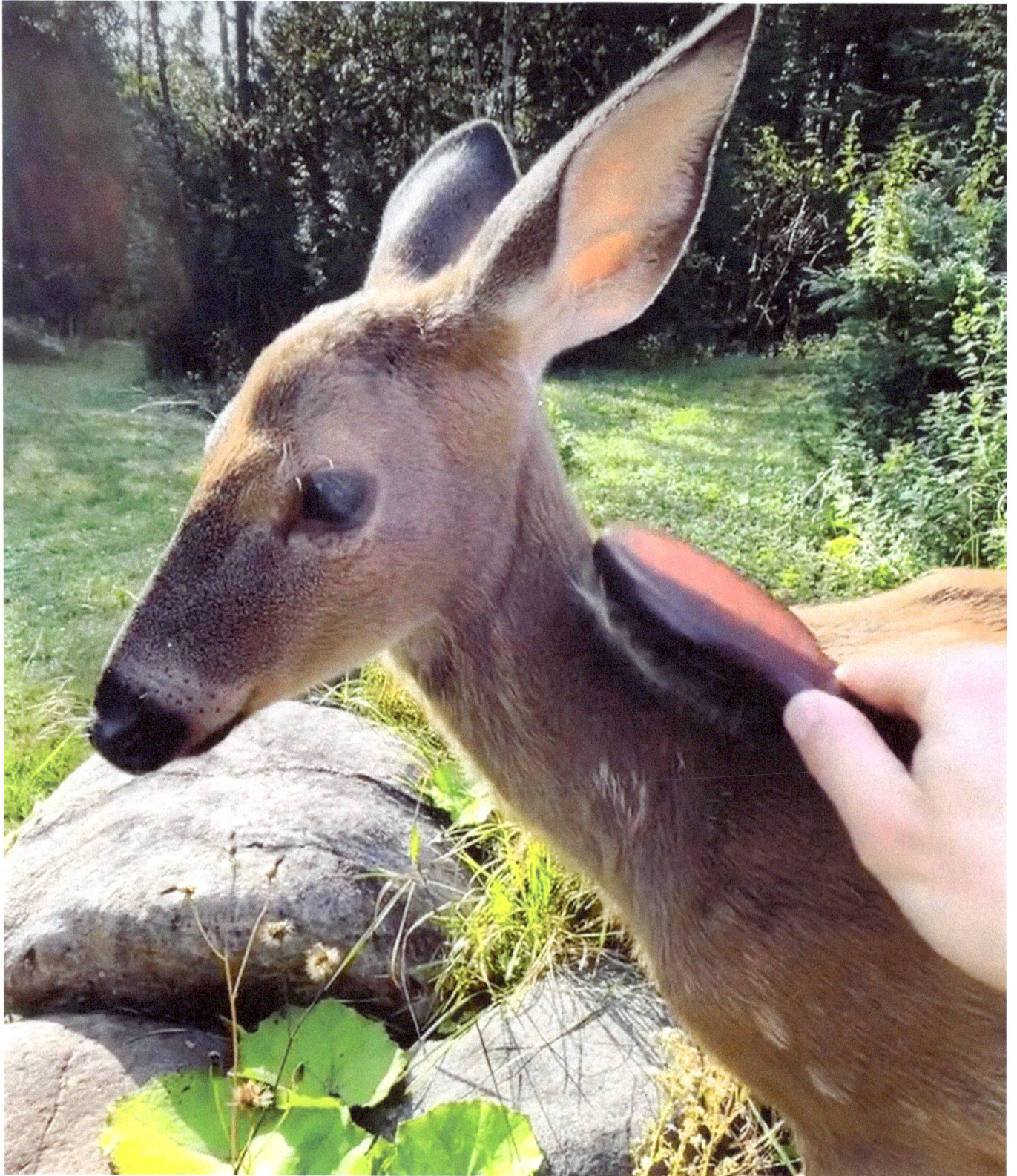

But summer was quickly fading into fall, with sudden sprinkles of rain and big gusts of wind. Fairy hid in the forest to protect herself as the weather worsened. Prince Jeff was concerned that Ontario would see a brutal winter with large accumulations of snow. "I must protect my precious Fairy," he thought. Because Fairy was so young and did not yet have her thick winter coat of fur,

Prince Jeff built her a wooden house with a wood-burning stove inside. Here, she could find warmth and protection after being out in the brutal wind, rain, cold, and snow. How wonderful, thought Fairy, to have this place of shelter.

*Jeff's dog also appreciated the cabin's warmth and the companionship of Fairy.*

Fairy eventually noticed Prince Jeff's castle. She seemed intrigued by it. "Could there be food inside?" she wondered.

Fairy wandered into the castle as soon as her Prince opened the door and whistled. After giving him an abundance of love and kisses, she noticed the house plants and thought, "I'll just take a little nibble from these delicious leaves!"

Then she trotted into his workout space. "What is this?" she wondered. "Oh, this must be how he keeps himself so physically fit. He needs to be strong to cut wood and build a shelter for me. Keep on working out Prince Jeff!" said Fairy.

Each day brought new and magical experiences. Fairy soon discovered that her prince was taking care of other animals. She met one of them through a castle window.

*"Who is this cute love ball?" asked Fairy. "I am Jocko, and my sister is Jenny," answered the raccoon. Fairy said, "I hope we get to meet outside and become one big, happy family!"*

"My amazing prince is creating a home for you guys!" said Fairy.
It looks like the love balls are helping to measure and cut the wood.

*Fairy thought the raccoons looked safe and warm in their new enclosure as the weather grew colder.*

19

"I see the prince has bought you a jungle gym," said Fairy. "It looks like fun!"

Fairy noticed that her prince was taking special care of Jenny.

"I heard he is giving you medicine, and that you are finally feeling better and eating. Soon you'll be healthy enough to go back out into the forest! You'll love that," said Fairy.

Fairy grew more curious with each passing moment. But even though her family was growing, Fairy was becoming lonely without other deer around. "Maybe I should join a herd," she thought. "I would love to meet some other animals like me." So Fairy wandered deep into the woods where she met Daisy, Felix, Finley, and Faith. Several times her new friends followed her to Prince Jeff's castle, where they saw Prince Jeff give food to Fairy. They thought, "He must be a good human since he feeds her; maybe he will feed us, too!" Sure enough, Prince Jeff scattered some food outside, close to his castle, and everyone ate.

The other deer could see that Fairy would be an asset to their herd, but they still were a bit hesitant to let her join them. They watched her from a distance, occasionally allowing Fairy to join them for some fun, and eventually they let her become a part of their family. Fairy learned from them some of the things that her mother would have taught her, like how to eat in nature. She learned to eat "browse," which is leaves, twigs, and buds, and "forbs," which are herbaceous flowering plants. Fairy especially enjoyed eating fruits, nuts, and seeds, or "mast" – she thought berries, apples, and acorns were the most delicious.

*It was exciting to see how much Fairy grew, and how she interacted more and more with her deer friends.*

As winter set in, the deer traveled deeper into the forest and their visits became fewer and farther between. Some days Prince Jeff put on his snowshoes and hiked far into the woods, searching for Fairy and looking for deer tracks. Prince Jeff loudly called her name and whistled for her. There was no response, but he felt confident that Fairy had become independent and that she was not alone. He knew that she was safe.

Prince Jeff was sure she would return in the spring, perhaps even with a fawn of her own. "You and I were meant to come into each other's lives, Fairy," said Prince Jeff. "You brought me joy, happiness, and peace, and I hope I did the same for you."

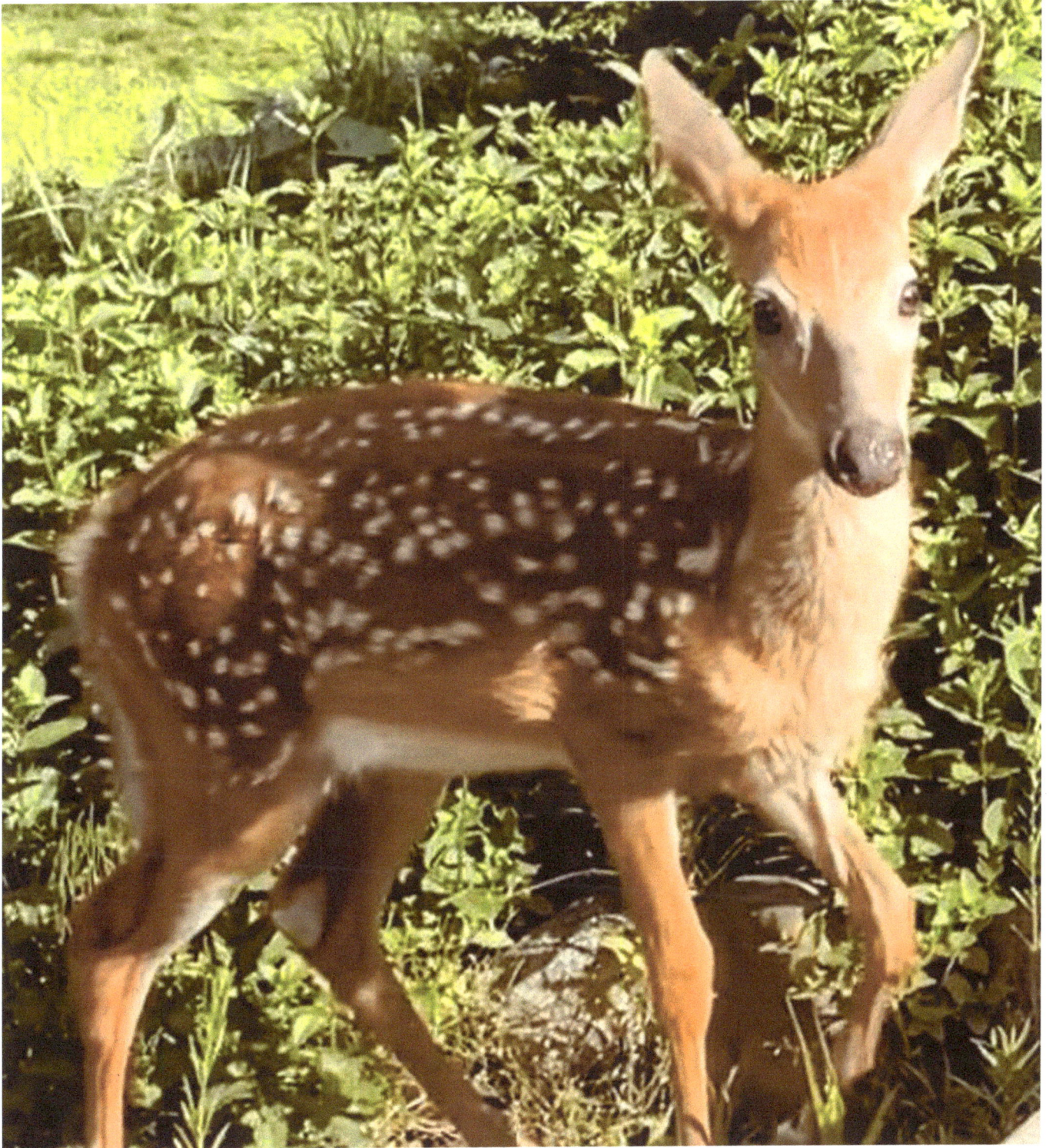

Prince Jeff wants all his friends to know that hunting and shooting deer are not acceptable. These are nature's beautiful creatures, just like our pet cats and dogs. Deer are loving, affectionate beings living their best lives in the wild, and we should not hurt them. We can also eat more foods that are plant-based, or even become vegan, so that instead of harming these beautiful animals to make our food, we help them to stay safe and protected.

"I love you, Fairy," says Jeff. "Until we meet again!"

# Moral of the Story

Be kind and caring to all species.
Show compassion to and help those in need.
Everyone deserves a chance to have a
wonderful life,
including wild animals.

# More Photos of Fairy and Friends

*Jeff created a stand to feed deer in his yard.*

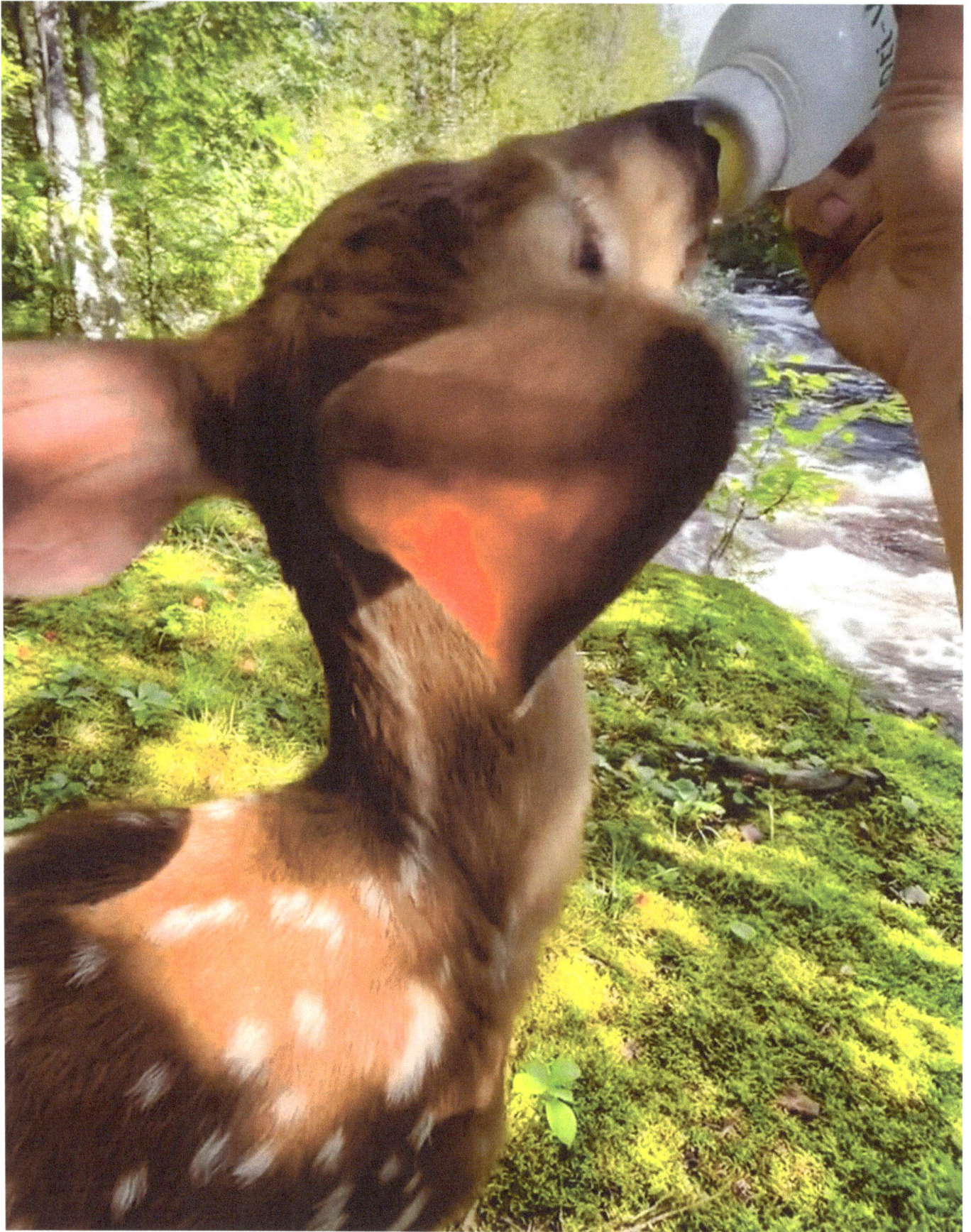

Jeff fed beautiful Fairy a nutritious plant-based milk formula.
On some days she drank as many as five or six bottles!

*Jeff, Fairy the fawn, Jeff's dog, and his raccoons,*
*Jenny and Jocko the love balls: one big, happy family.*

31

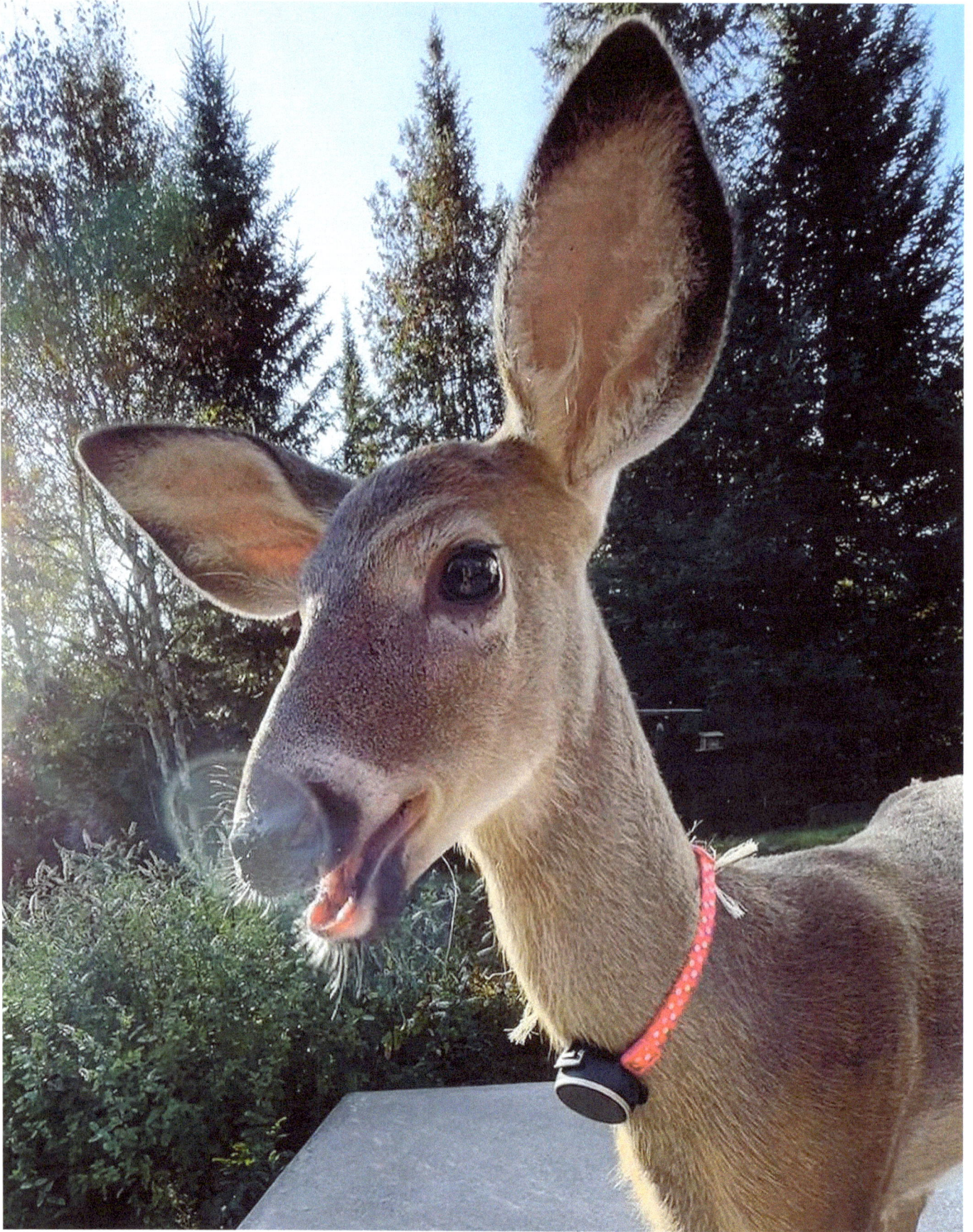

*Jeff kept Fairy safe during hunting season;*
*he tracked her whereabouts when she wandered in the forest.*

*Fairy could feel Jeff's care and love.*

*Jeff and Fairy shared an undeniable bond.*

*Jeff and Fairy enjoying some snuggle time.*

*Even as an adult, Fairy still enjoyed being brushed.*

36

# Educational Facts & Activities

# Fun Fawn Facts

1. Fawns weigh 4–8 pounds at birth.
2. Fawns that reach one-and-a-half months to two months old can survive on their own without their mom.
3. Fawns are born about 200 days after mating.
4. Fawns will stand within minutes after being born, and walk within hours.
5. Does need to find food, so they leave their fawns alone for extended periods during the day. The moms find safe spots near rivers, streams, or lakes, or in tall vegetation, so the babies will not be spotted by predators.
6. The white camouflage spots on a fawn's fur fade away as the deer matures.
7. Deer have eyes on the sides of their head to give them a wide field of vision to watch out for predators.
8. Deer are herbivores, which means they eat only plants.
9. Deer love carrots.
10. Fawns and does check you out from afar. They may remember you by your smell, appearance, and voice.
11. A doe will not abandon her fawns, but she will leave them alone for long periods of time, especially in May, June, and July, in order to keep predators from seeing her and knowing her vulnerable baby is nearby.
12. Fawns drink their mom's milk for approximately four to five months.
13. At three or four months, fawns begin to eat more vegetation.
14. Fawns have a way of communicating when in danger or when looking for their moms. It's called a "bleat." It sounds like they are crying.
15. If a doe has twin or triplet fawns, she keeps them in different spots to nurse them, and she separates them when they're left alone. She feels it is safer and not as likely to attract predators.
16. Fawns weigh approximately 60–70 pounds by their first winter.
17. Does nurse their newborn fawns approximately four times a day.
18. Deer stay warm in the winter by growing a thick, wooly undercoat of fur.
19. At night, deer may be seen in more-populated areas.
20. The average life expectancy of male white-tailed deer is about six years, and eight years for females.
21. Does who are one year old can have a fawn. When does are two or older, they are more likely to have twins or even triplets.
22. Female fawns remain with their mom for a year and stay nearby after that, while male fawns leave after a year.
23. Most deer sleep during the day. They eat very early in the morning, during the evening, and late at night.
24. Deer stomp when they perceive a threat and want to warn other deer.
25. White-tailed deer can sprint at speeds of up to 35 or 40 miles per hour, and they can maintain a speed of 25 miles per hour for three to four miles.

# Emotions/Feelings

Who felt this way: Prince Jeff, Fairy, or both? When in the story did you notice Prince Jeff or Fairy showing the feeling?

**Scared**

**Lonely**

**Distraught**

**Sad**

**Afraid**

**Grateful**

**Happy**

**Content**

**Joyful**

**Fulfilled**

**Kind**

**Compassionate**

**Caring**

**Altruistic**

# Sentence Starters

1. When Fairy and Prince Jeff met, I felt _____
   because _____
2. When Fairy was all alone, I felt _____ because _____
3. I think Fairy was an orphan because _____
4. I fell in love with Fairy because _____
5. Fairy and Prince Jeff _____

# Reading Comprehension

1. What would have made this story more interesting to read?
2. Would people in your family help animals in need?
3. Can you come up with another title for this story?
4. Did anything surprise you in this story?
5. How do you think Prince Jeff felt during hunting season?
6. What are some reasons why an animal may need rehabilitation?
7. What are your thoughts on being a vegan?
8. Do you think there are good non-animal ways to eat protein?
9. Do you think animals deserve a second chance at life? Why or why not?
10. What do you think the biggest danger is to a deer?
11. Do you think Fairy will come back to visit during the warmer seasons?
12. Do you think Fairy will remember her rehabilitator, Prince Jeff?
13. Do you think the other deer were receptive right away to having Fairy join their herd? Please explain.
14. After reading this story, how do you feel about deer hunting?
15. Do you think Fairy will come back alone or with other deer? Please explain.
16. Do you think Prince Jeff should have kept Fairy with humans instead of setting her free?

# "WH" Questions

**WHO**

1. Who is this story about?
2. Who did Fairy meet at the beginning of the story?
3. Who did Fairy leave with at the end of the story?

**WHAT**

1. What did Prince Jeff do to show kindness?
2. What did Prince Jeff do to keep Fairy alive?
3. What did Prince Jeff do to keep Fairy warm?
4. What led Prince Jeff to think Fairy was orphaned?

**WHEN**

1. When did Fairy meet Prince Jeff? (Name the season.)
2. When did Fairy leave Prince Jeff? (Name the season.)
3. When an animal is rehabilitated, should it be kept as a pet? Why or why not?
4. When is it safe to interact with a wild animal?
5. When do deer come into populated areas?

**WHERE**

1. Where do deer live?
2. Where did the story take place?
3. Where do you think Fairy went at the end of the story?

**WHY**

1. Why was Prince Jeff kind to Fairy?
2. Why did Fairy allow Prince Jeff to feed her?
3. Why did Fairy allow Prince Jeff to brush her fur?
4. Why did Fairy leave at the end of the story?

# Vocabulary Development

Here are some of the words and phrases from this story, along with their definitions. Can you create a sentence with each of these?

1. **Majestic**/magical
2. **Fawn**/baby deer
3. **Tragedy**/accident
4. **Wilderness**/natural outdoors
5. **Lush**/lots of greenery
6. **Rehabilitation**/restoring to health
7. **Orphaned**/all alone
8. **Magnificent**/wonderful
9. **Inseparable**/always together
10. **Innocent**/pure
11. **Scent**/smell
12. **Enticing**/tempting or desirable
13. **Ravenous**/starving
14. **Luscious**/delicious
15. **Emanate**/give out or emit
16. **Trot**/fast pace or running
17. **Hesitant**/not sure
18. **Stroked**/petted
19. **Pure heaven**/wonderful
20. **Brutal**/harmful
21. **Castle**/big house where royalty lives
22. **Wandered**/moving around; exploring
23. **Herd of deer**/deer in a group
24. **Blizzard**/snowstorm
25. **Vegan**/a person who does not eat food derived from animals
26. **Affectionate**/caring
27. **Protected**/caregiver won't allow harm
28. **Doe**/female deer
29. **Fawn**/baby deer
30. **Hoof**/foot of a deer or horse
31. **Rehabilitator**/someone who helps injured or sick animals return to good health

# Venn Diagram

Draw two circles that intersect one another. Label the two outside circles as differences. The small area of overlap will be their similarities. For example, work on the similarities and differences of:

1. A dog and a deer.

2. A moose and a deer.

3. A person and a deer.

4. Continue comparing and contrasting a deer to other animals such as a bison, a giraffe, a moose, an antelope, a zebra, and more.

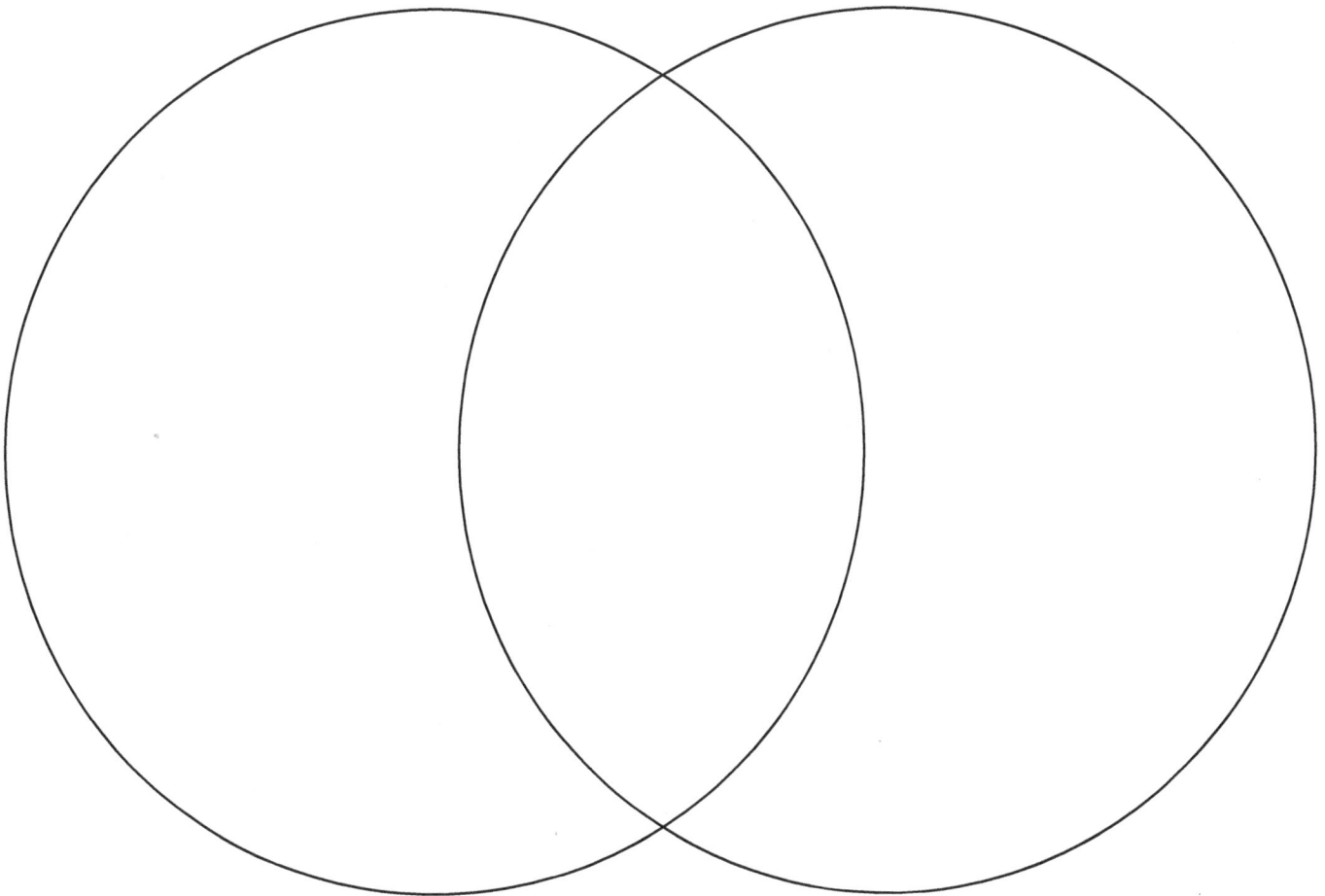

# Jokes

1. **How do you show affection to a deer?**
   *You fawn over her.*

2. **Why do deer need braces?**
   *They have buck teeth.*

3. **Where can a deer get cafe lattes and coffee?**
   *At Starbucks.*

4. **How much does a coffee cost?**
   *Under a buck.*

5. **What game do fawns like to play with their friends?**
   *Truth or deer.*

6. **What should the deer order for dessert?**
   *Cookie doe and doe-nuts.*

7. **Name a favorite song.**
   *Do-Re-Mi (Doe, a deer, a female deer...)*

8. **If a deer works, how should you pay him?**
   *Pay him with doe (dough = money)*

| | | |
|---|---|---|
| **F** | **Friendship** | Develop a deep feeling of friendship for animals in the wild. |
| **A** | **Altruism** | Selfless concern for taking care of animals. |
| **I** | **Illuminating** | Gain more insight into wildlife. |
| **R** | **Respect** | Respect the rights of animals. |
| **Y** | **Yearning** | Learn to have a deep yearning for the well-being of wildlife. |

Milton Keynes UK
Ingram Content Group UK Ltd.
UKHW050006260524
443026UK00004B/44

9 798869 270139